24
Three-Part Inventions
for piano

*

Traumear

Paperback ISBN 978-0-244-67221-8

*

www.traumear.com

Index

Inv.	pg.
1	1
2	4
3	8
4	11
5	15
6	13
7	19
8	22
9	30
10	33
11	38
12	42
13	45
14	49
15	53
16	56
17	60
18	67
19	72
20	76
21	80
22	85
23	89
24	93

*

Invention I

Traumear

Invention II

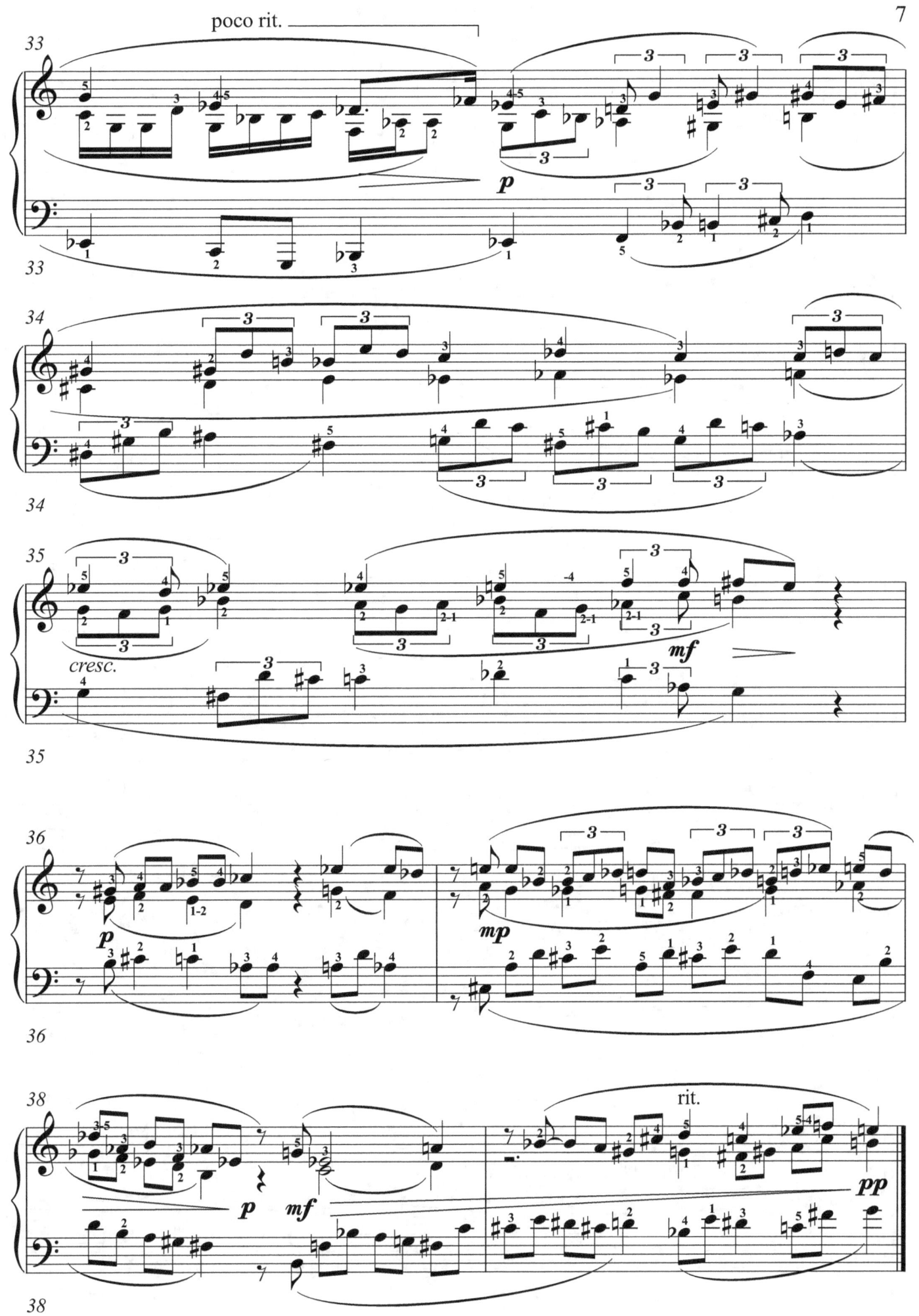

Invention III

Invention IV

12

Invention V

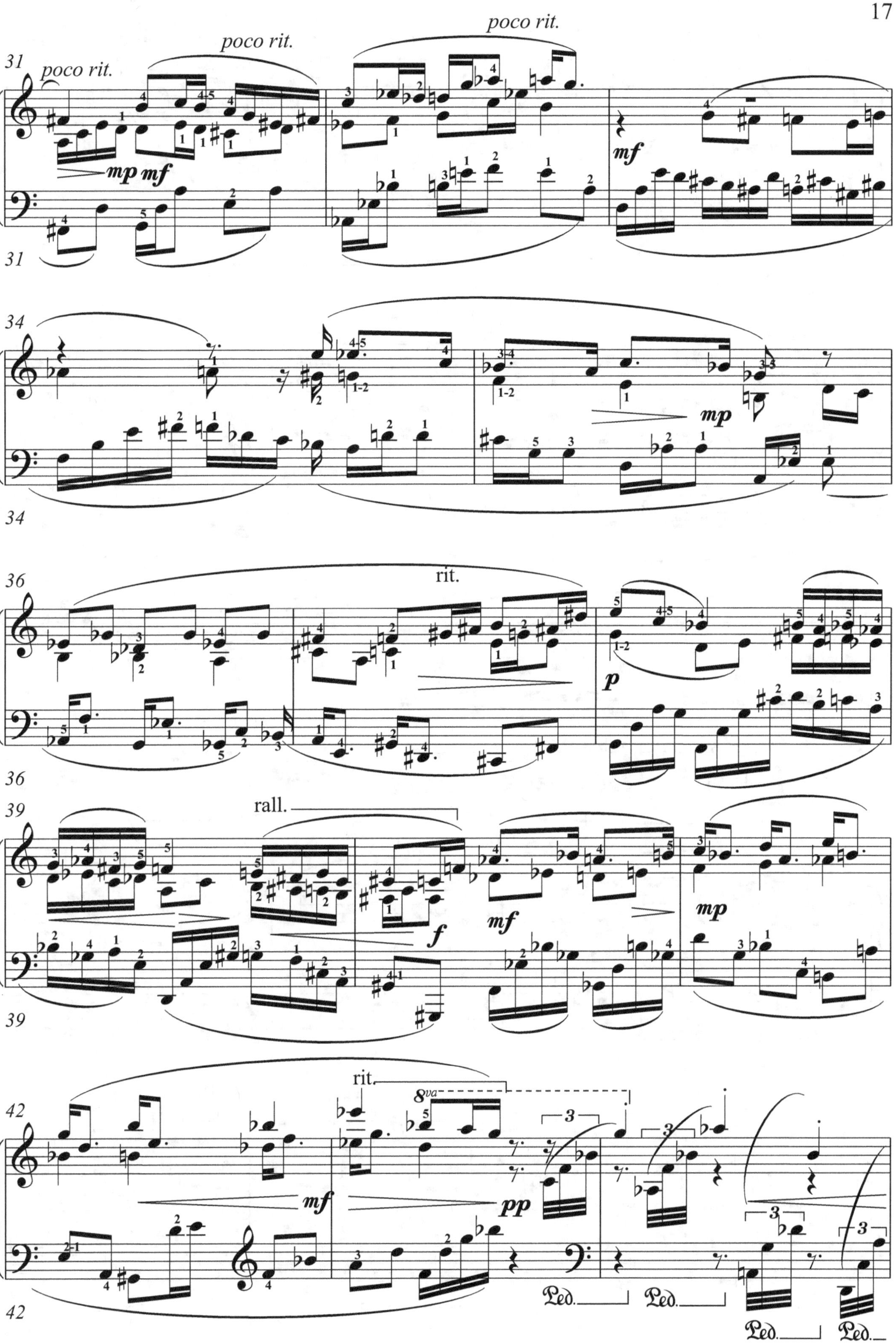
31
poco rit.
poco rit.
poco rit.
mp
mf
mf
34
mp
36
rit.
p
39
rall.
f
mf
mp
42
rit.
8va
mf
pp
Ped.
Ped.
Ped.
Ped.

Invention VI

Invention VII

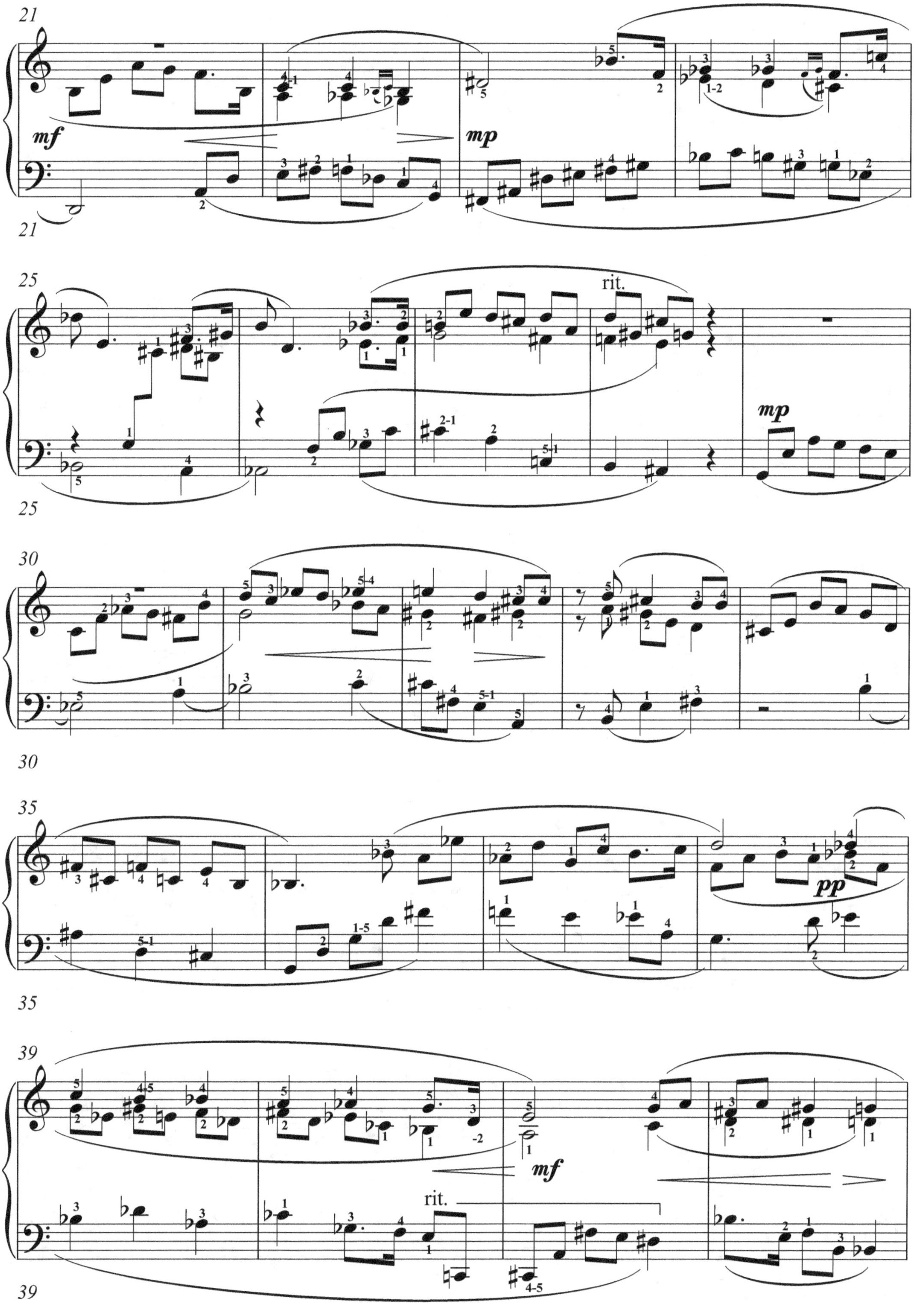
21
mf
mp
25
rit.
mp
30
35
pp
39
rit.
mf

Invention VIII

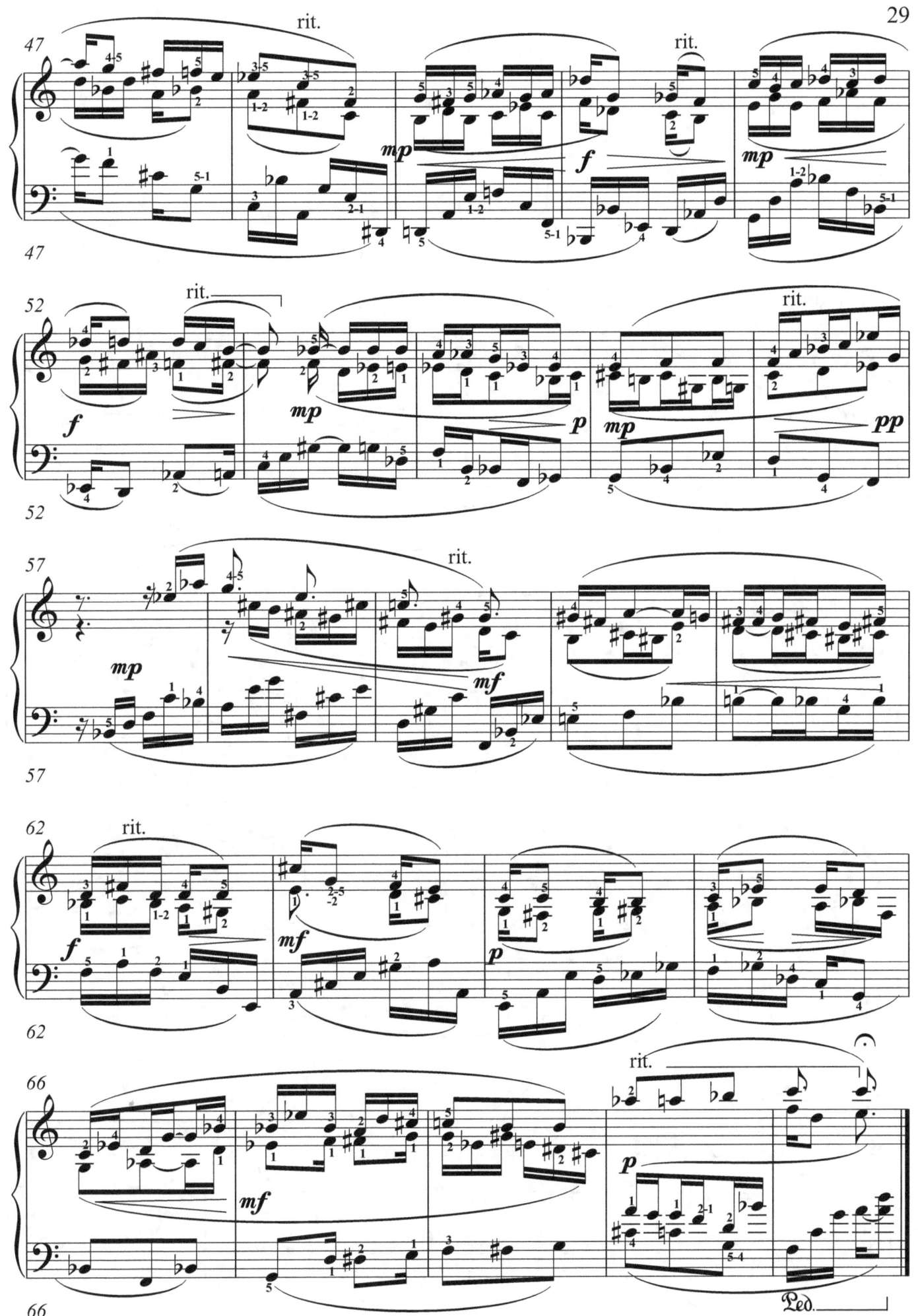

Invention IX

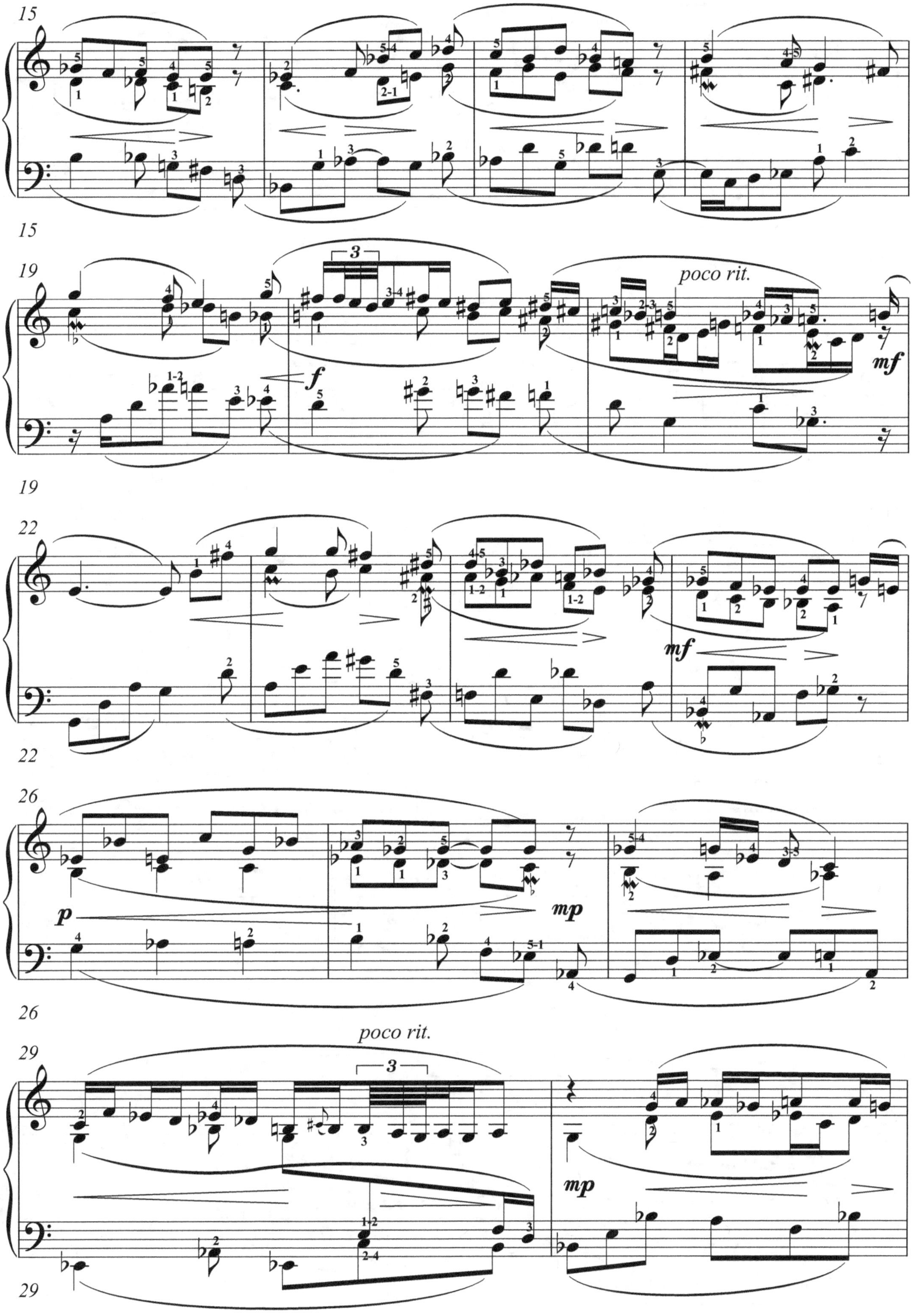
15
19
poco rit.
f
mf
22
mf
26
p
mp
29
poco rit.
mp

Invention X

Invention XI

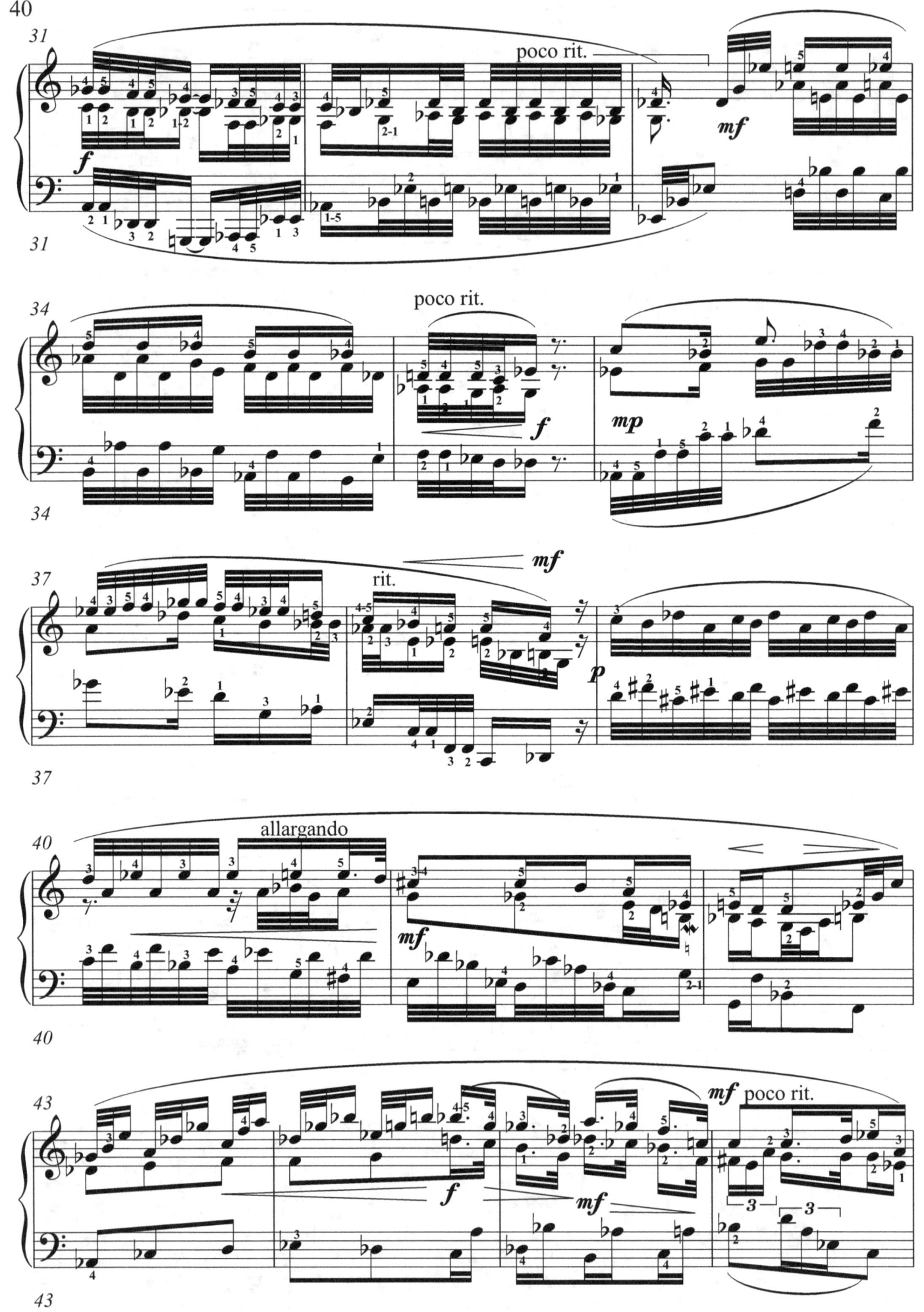

Invention XII

Invention XIII

Invention XIV

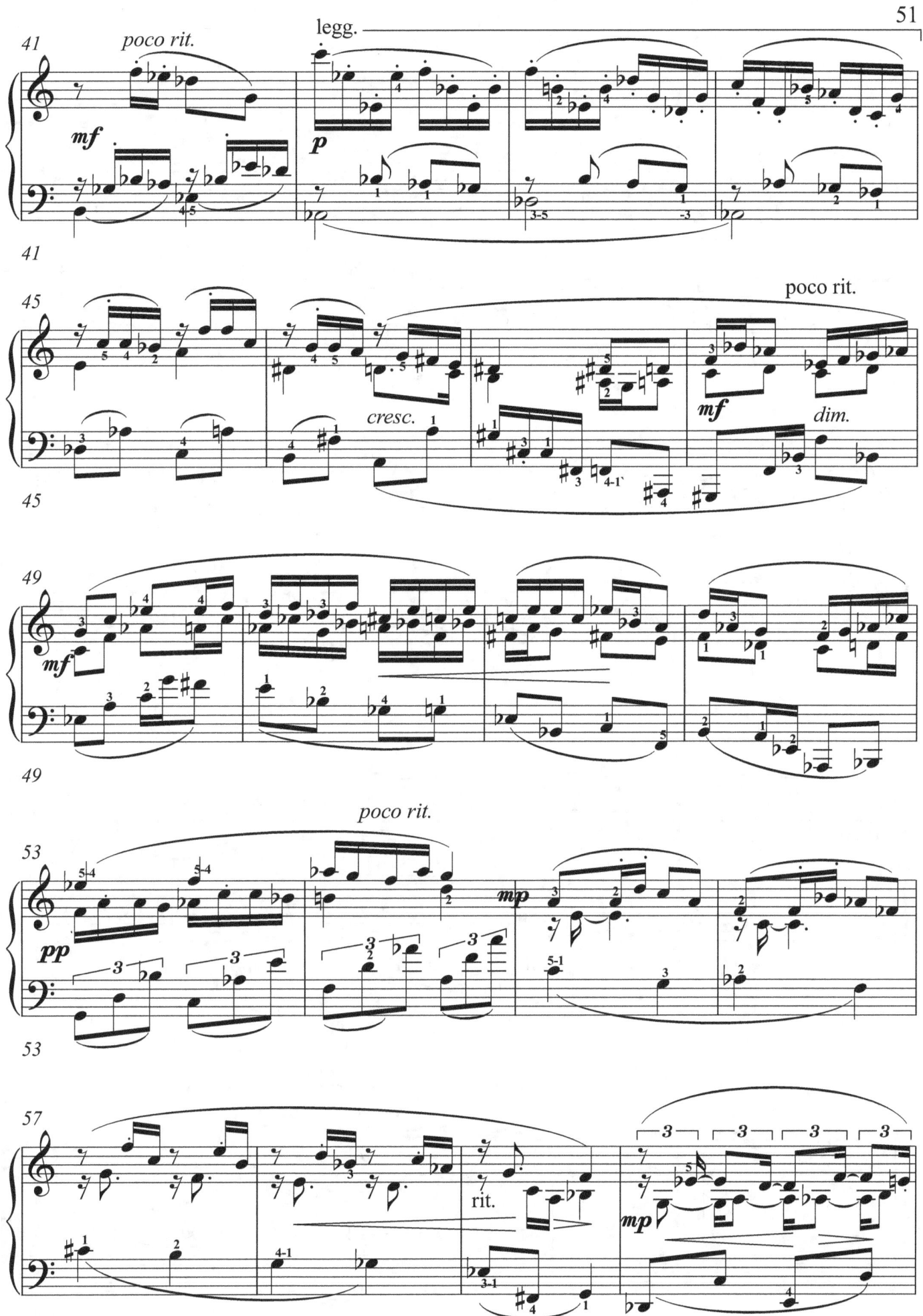

52

Invention XV

Invention XVI

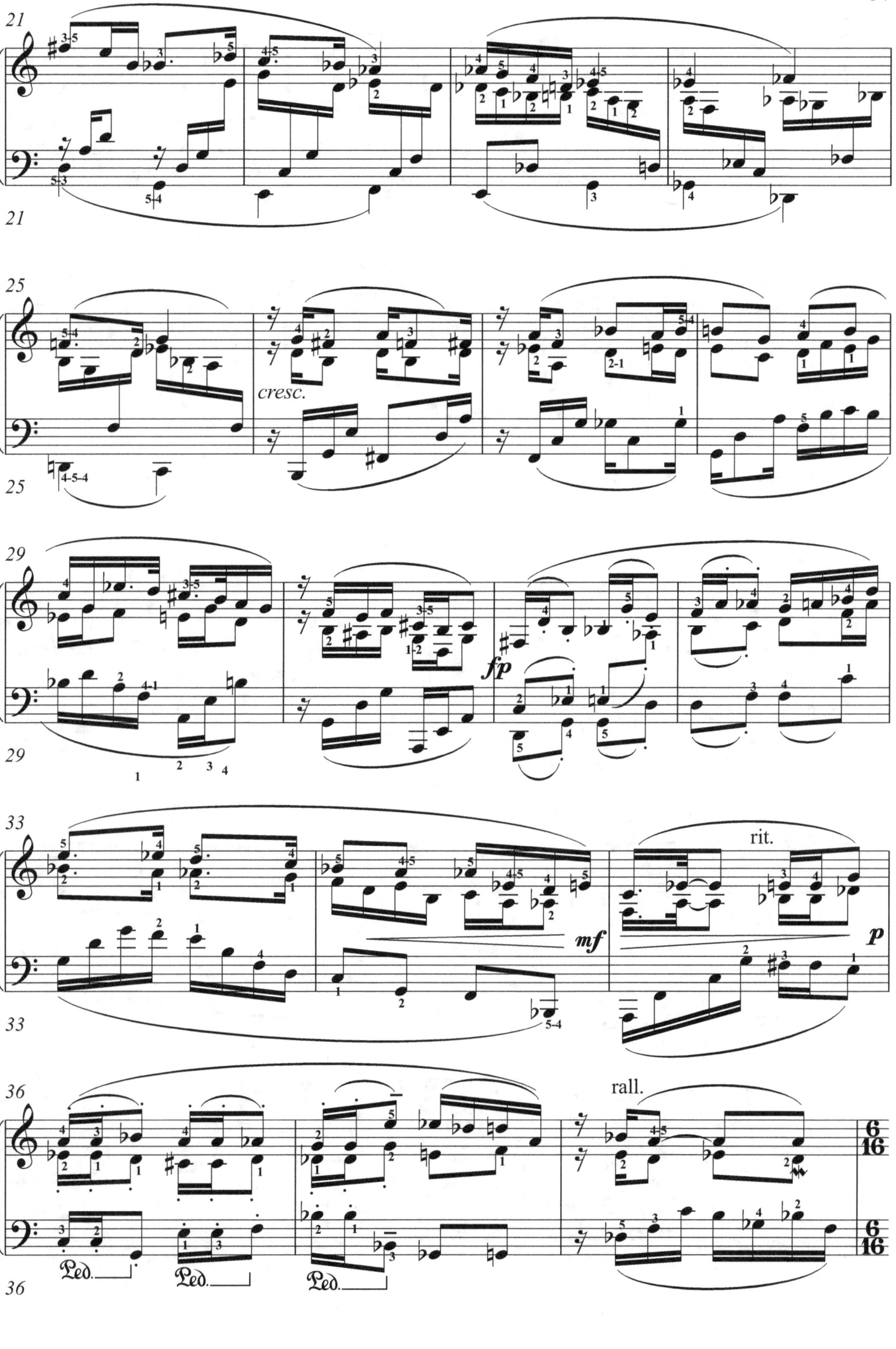
21
25
cresc.
29
fp
33
mf
rit.
p
36
rall.
Ped.
Ped.
Ped.

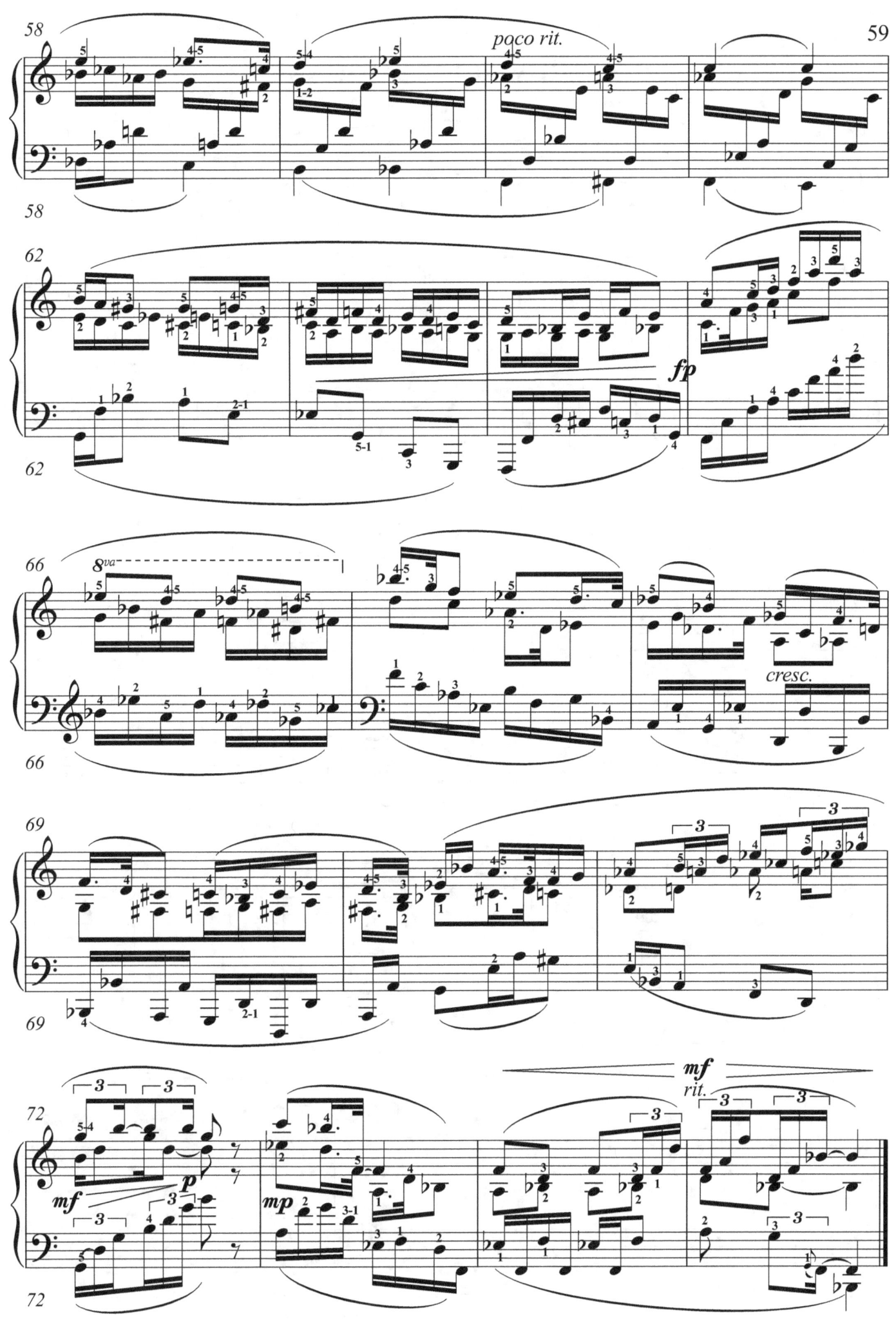

Invention XVII

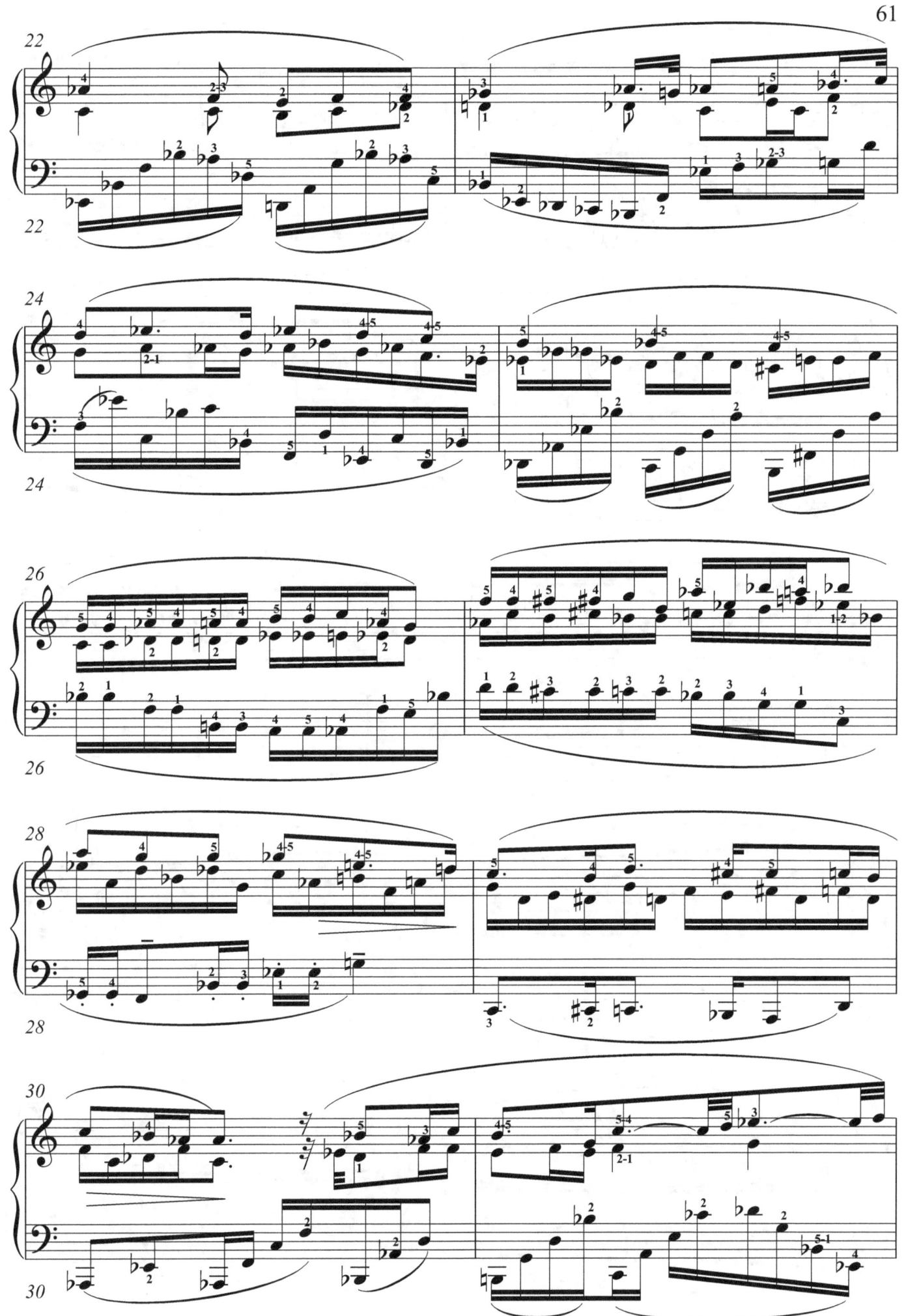

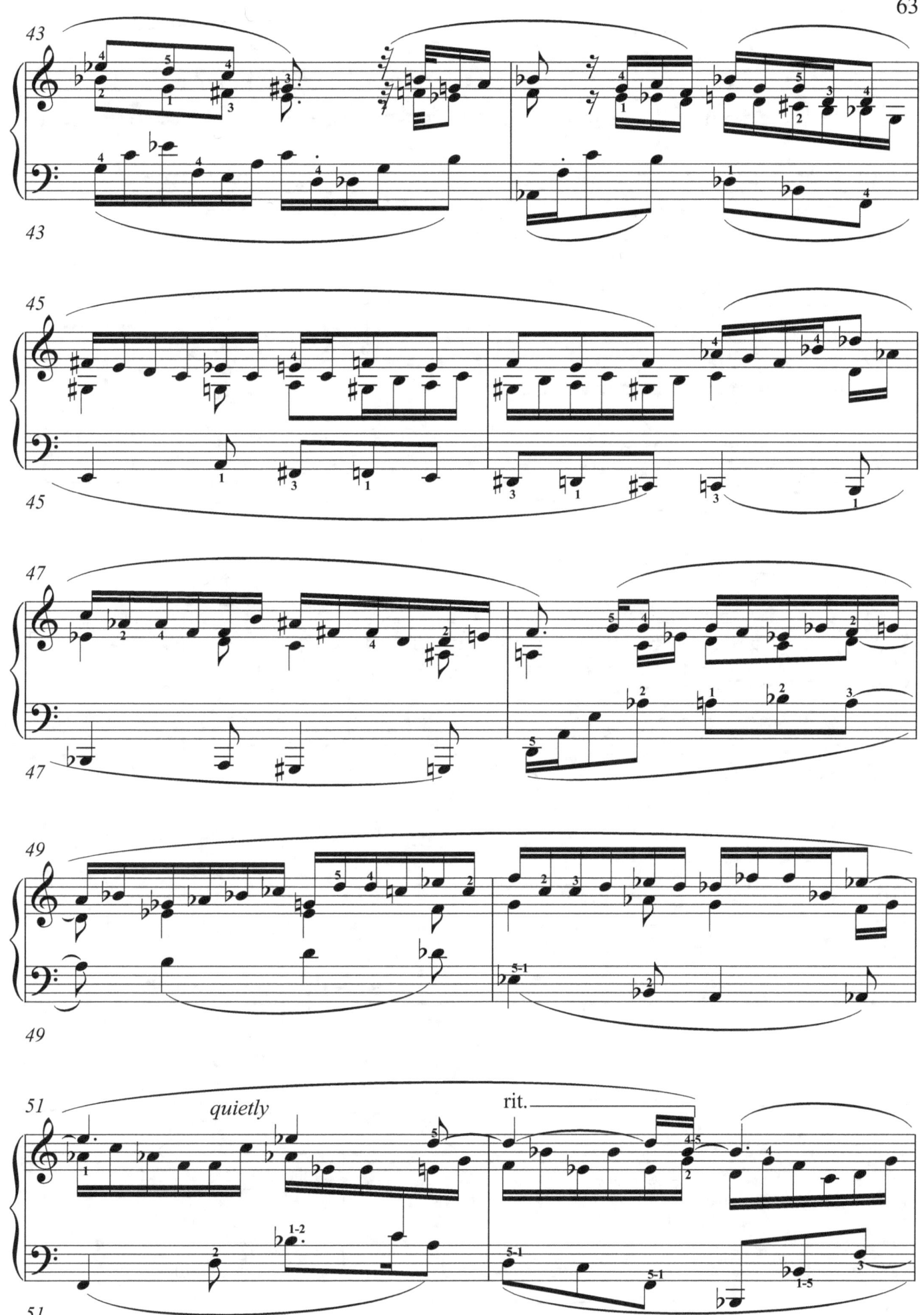

66

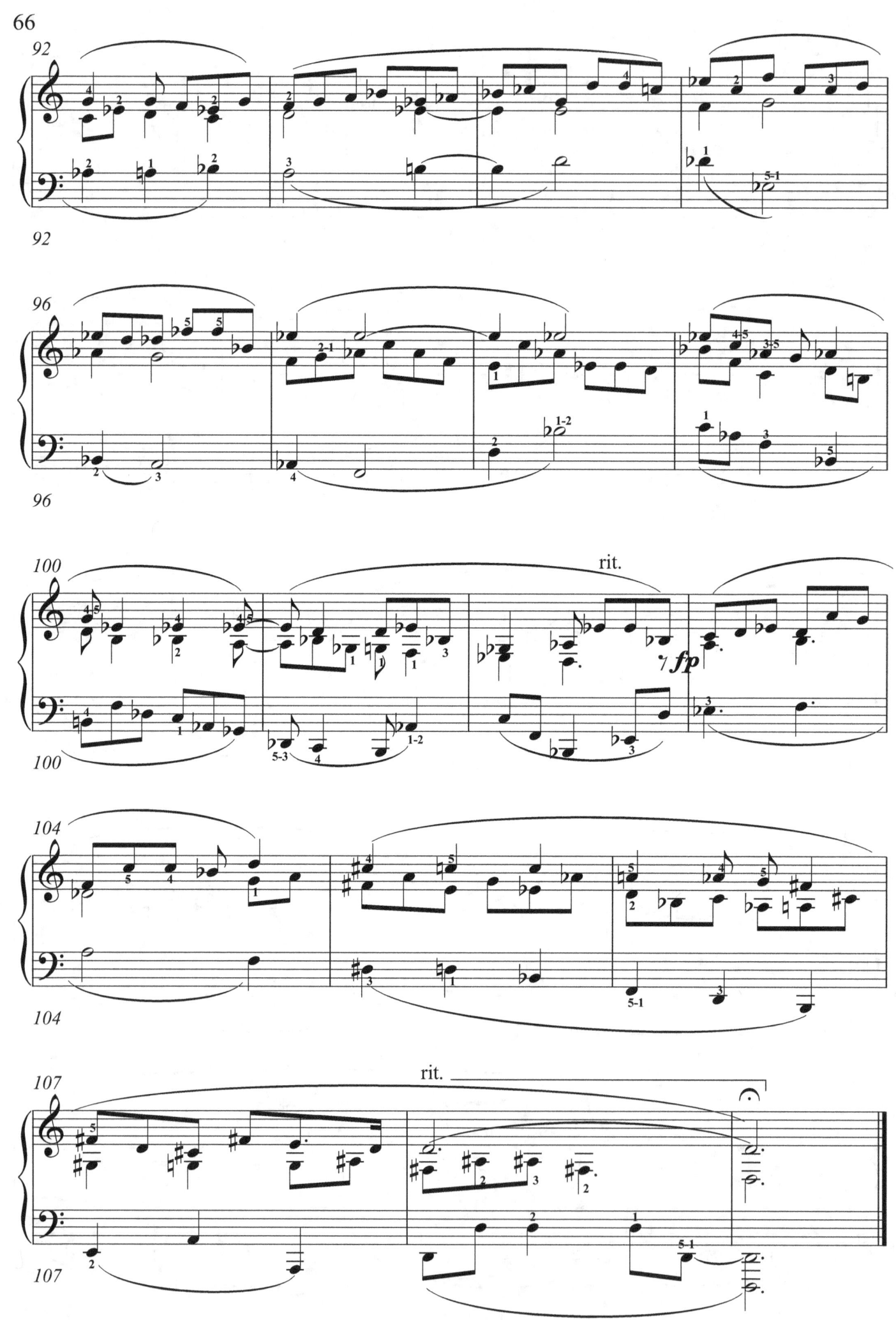

Invention XVIII

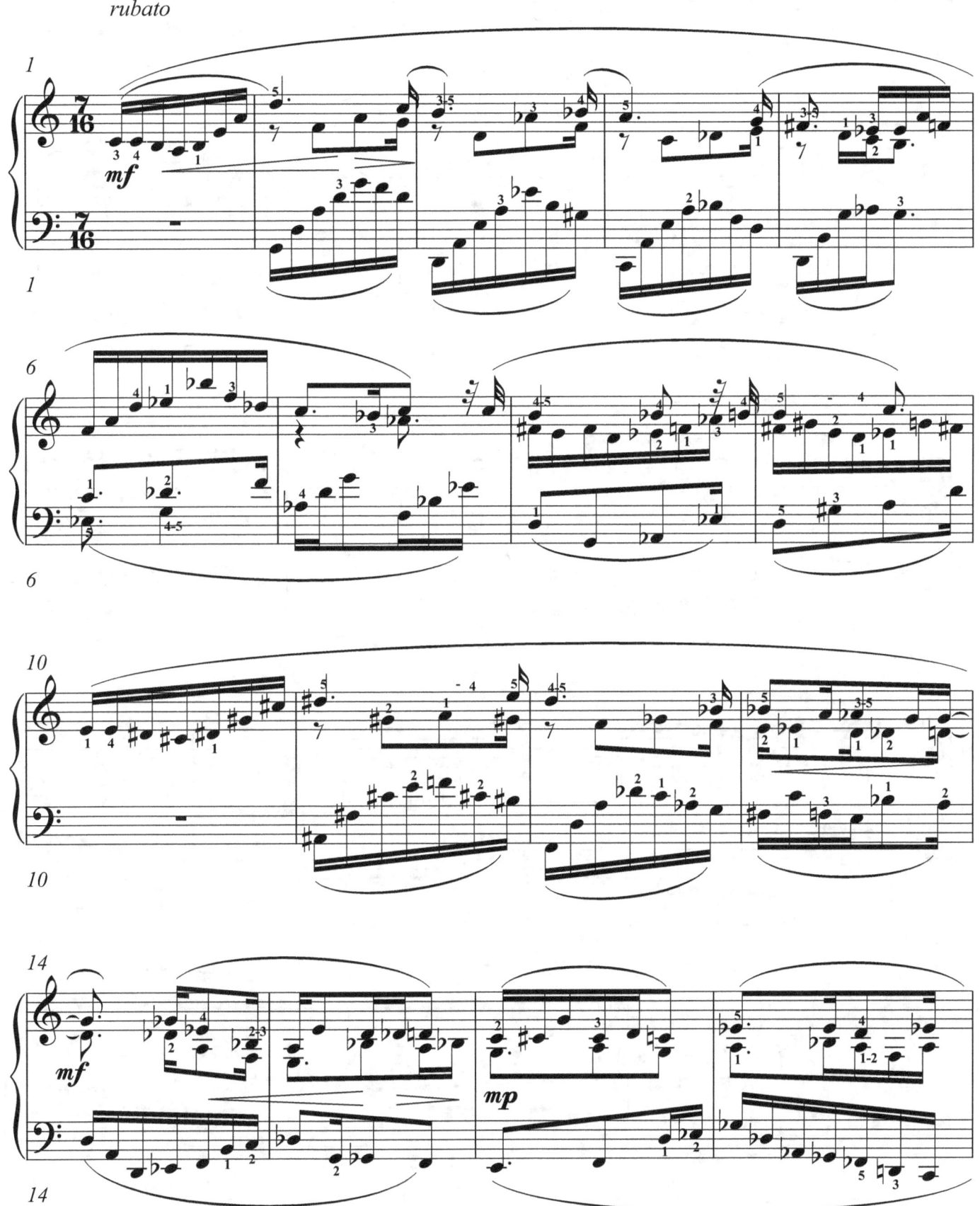

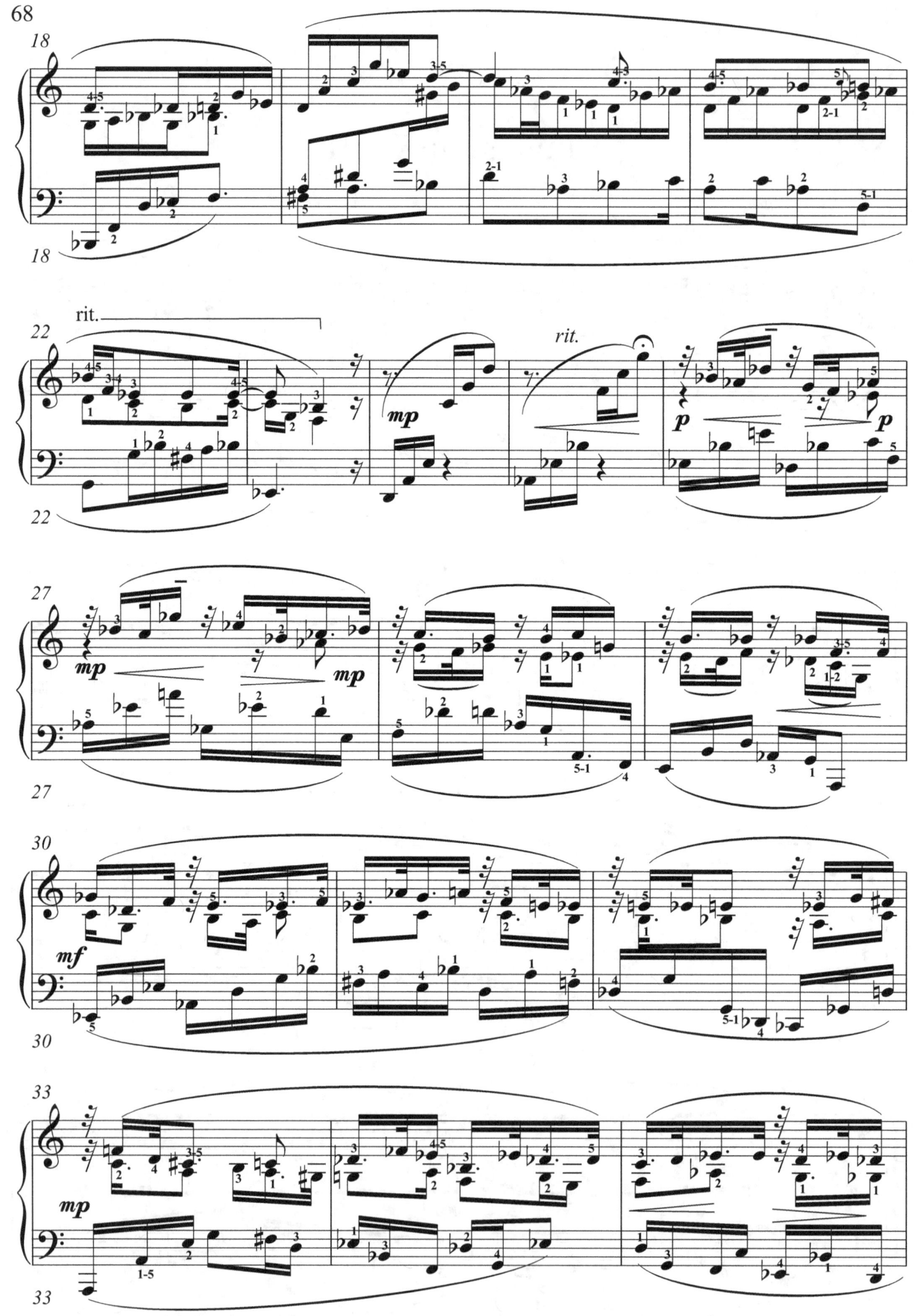

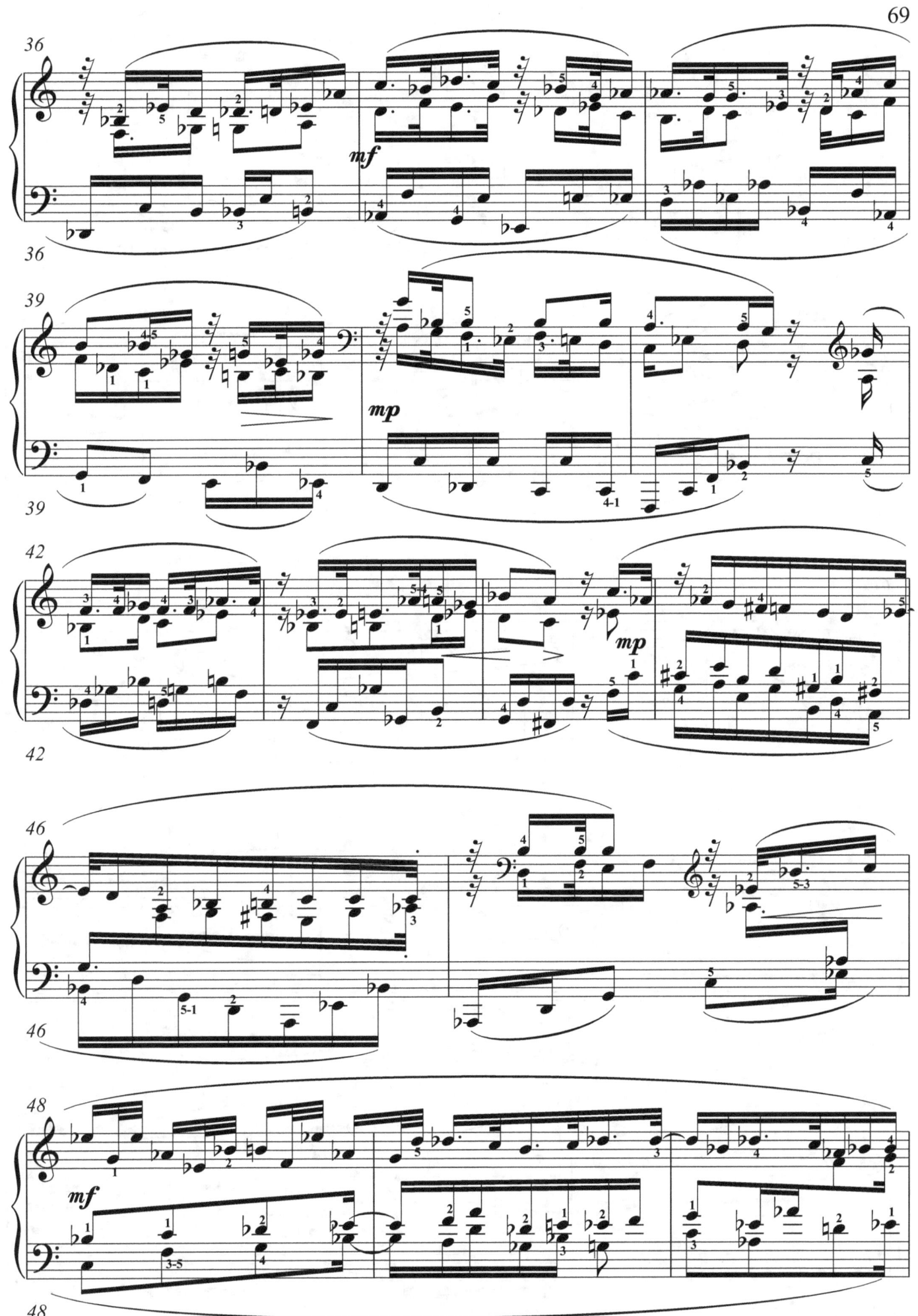

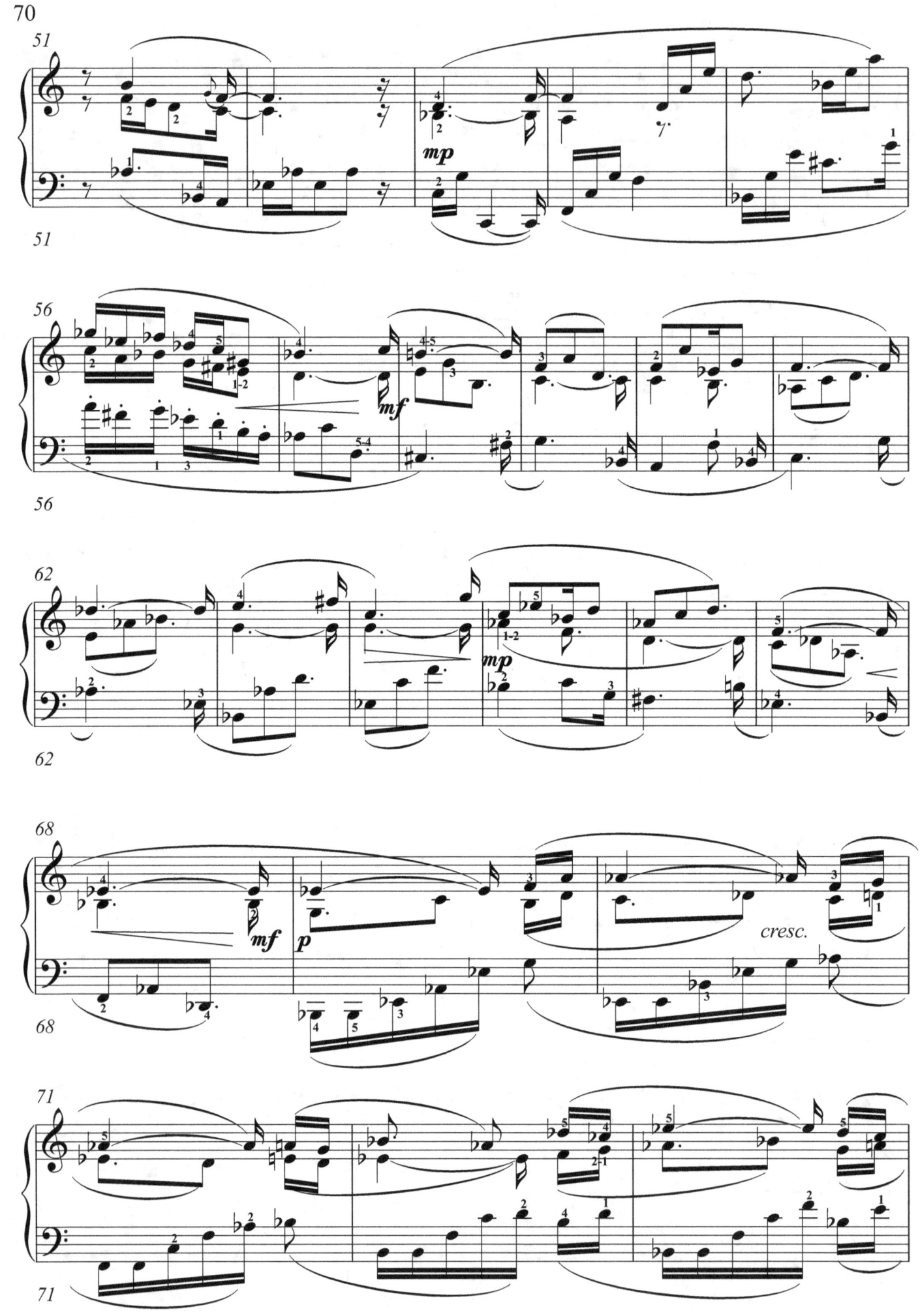

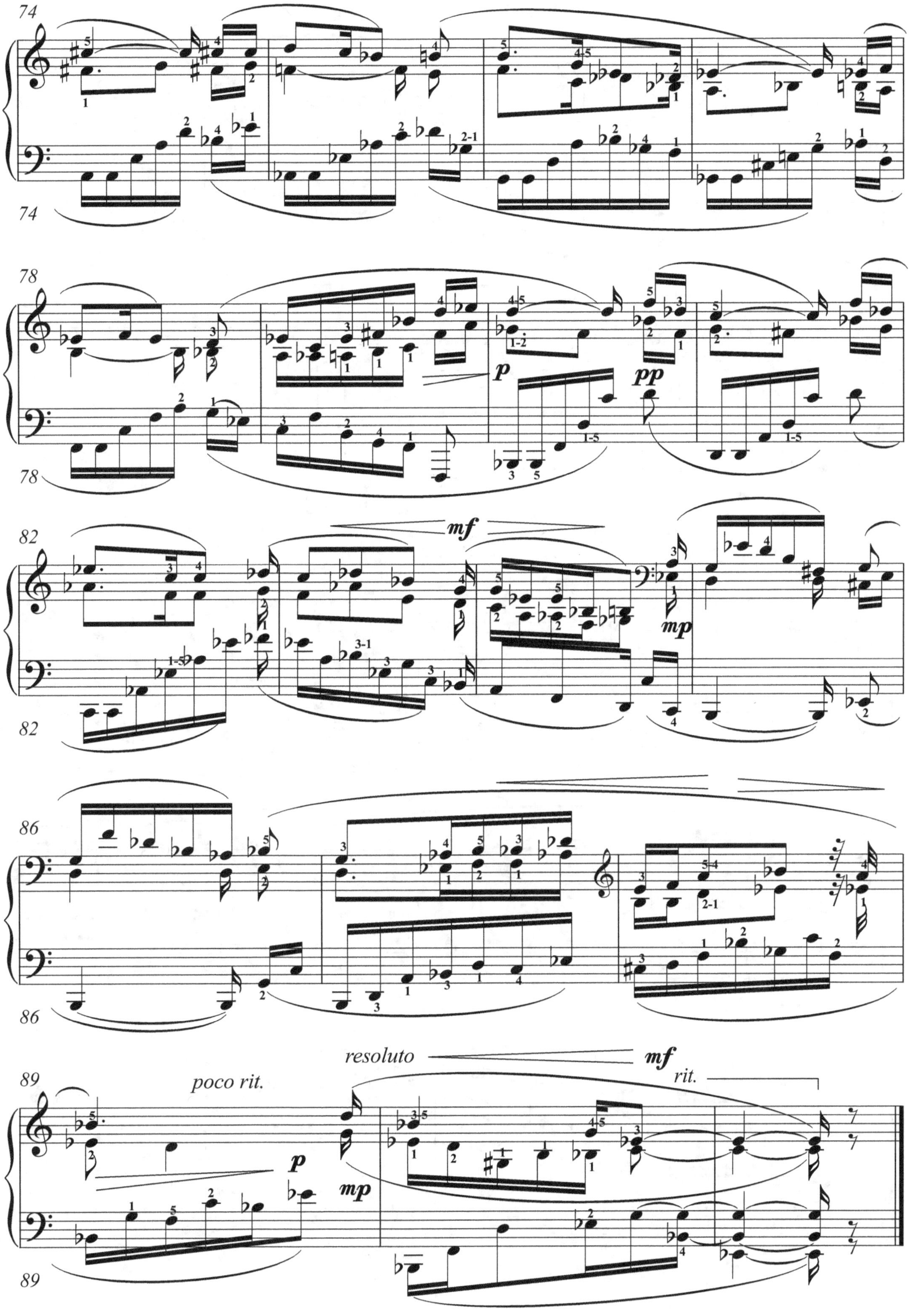
74
78
82
86
89
p
pp
mf
mp
resoluto
poco rit.
rit.

Invention XIX

Invention XX

Invention XXI

2:07'44.1"
4.1.73
Hit 01

poco rit.

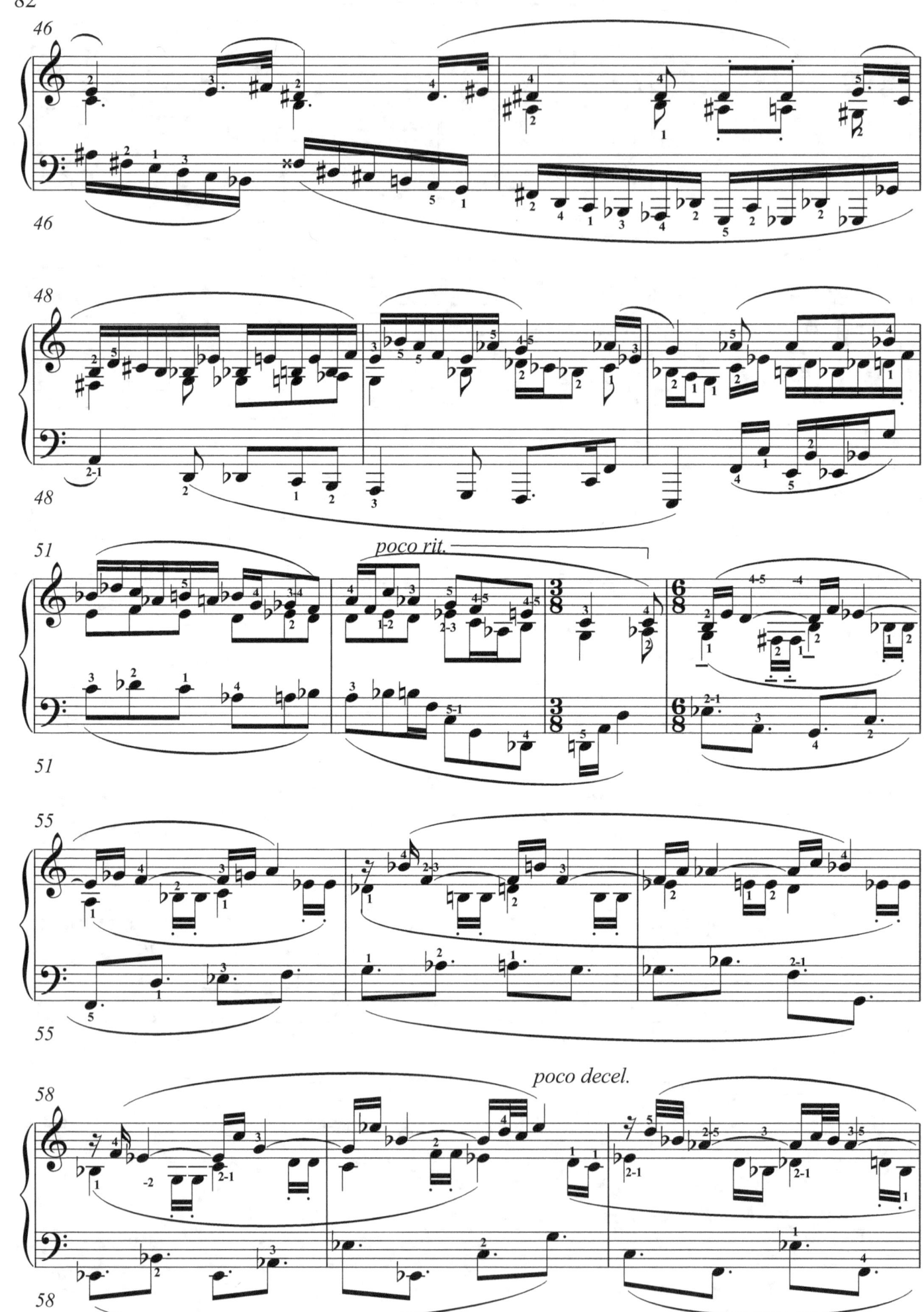

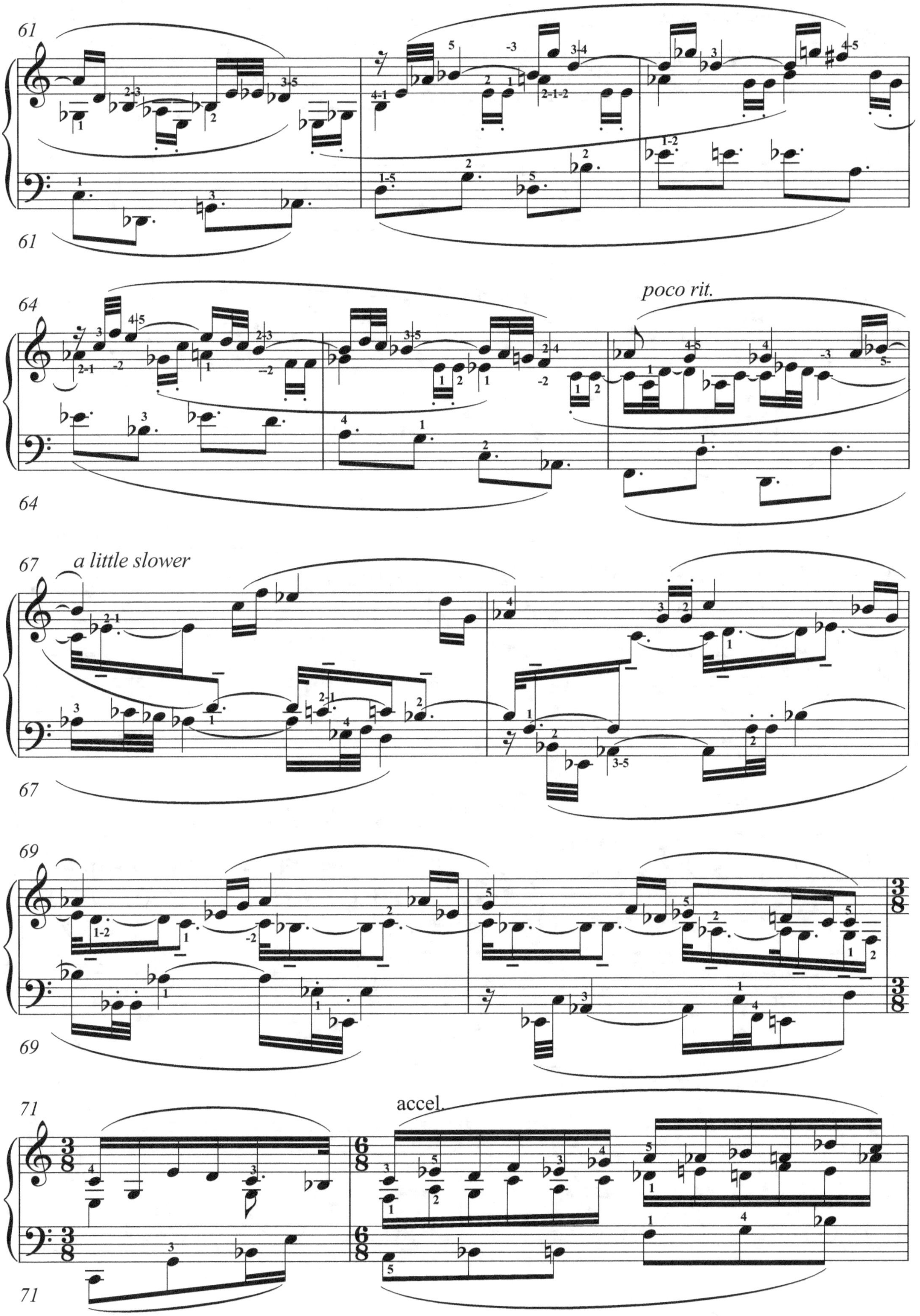
61
61
64
poco rit.
64
67
a little slower
67
69
69
71
accel.
71

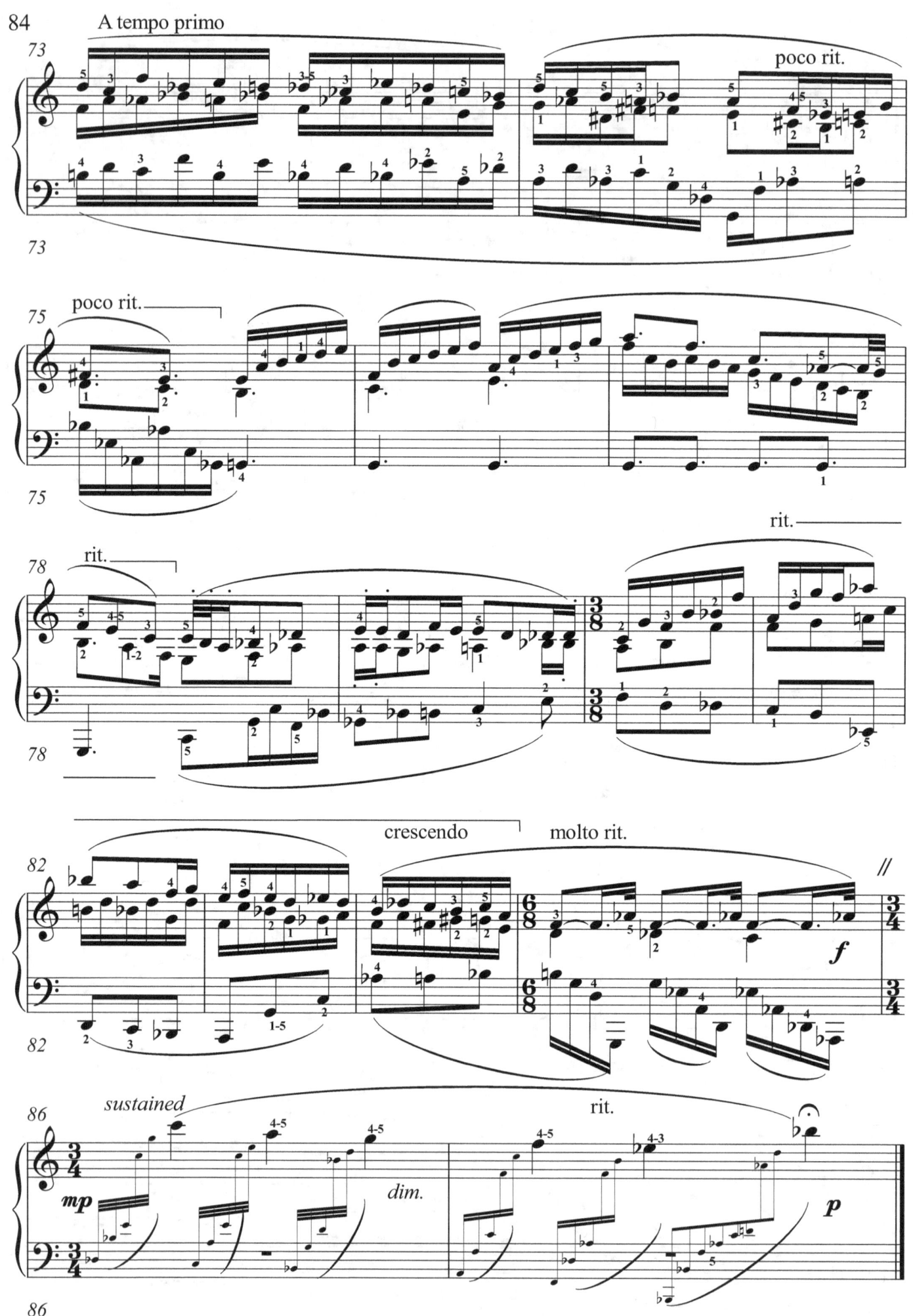

Invention XXII

Moderato, rubato

Three Part Invention XXIII

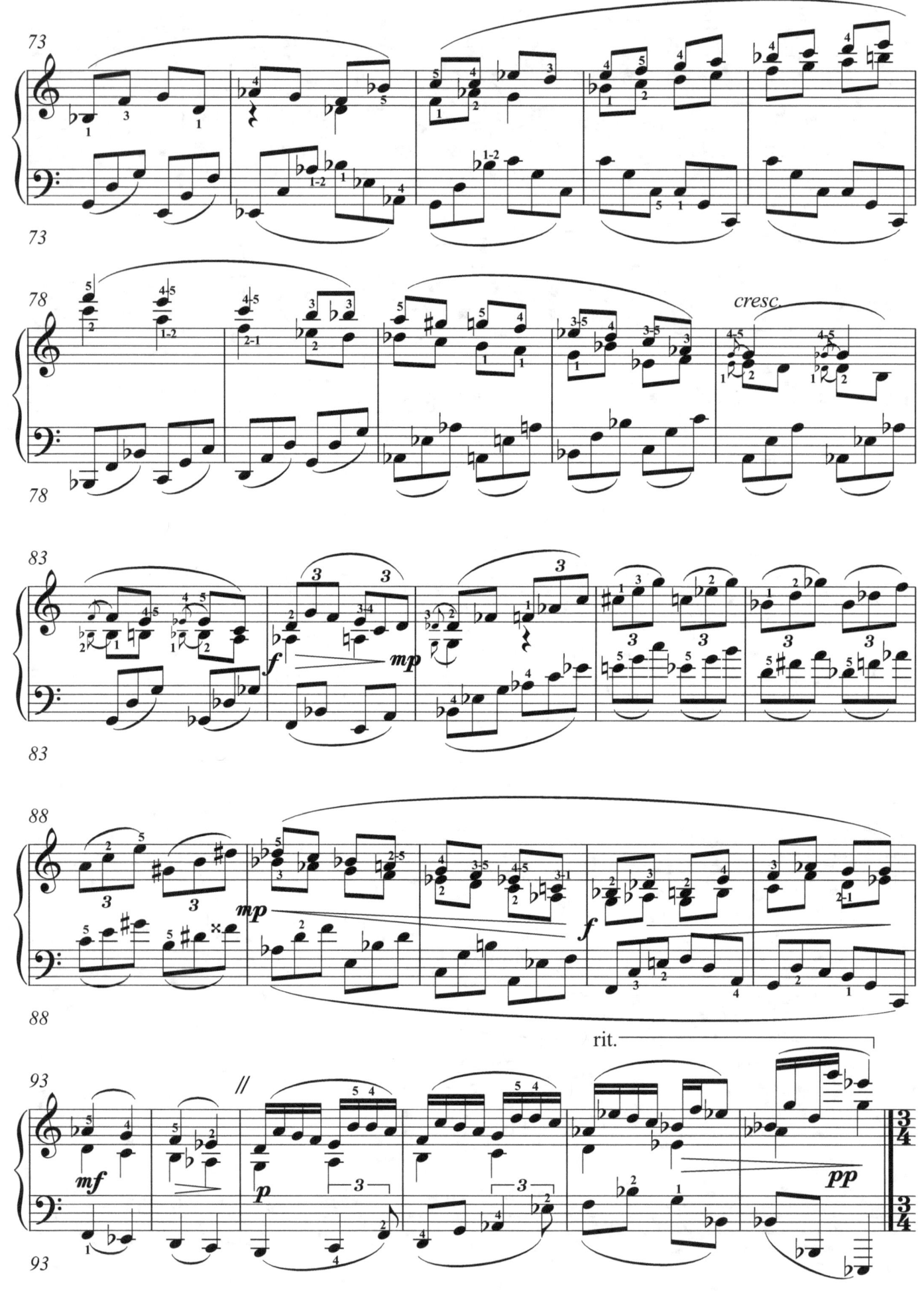

Three Part Invention XXIV

www.ingramcontent.com/pod-product-compliance
Lightning Source LLC
Chambersburg PA
CBHW081202280526
45791CB00006B/2157